Exercises in English
(2)
Vocabulary Extension

About the Author

Wendy Ijioma is an internationally renowned Teacher and Author who has dedicated more than 50 years to educating thousands of non-native English speakers in the finer points of the English language. Her career in teaching began at the village school in Glinton, Cambridgeshire followed by Teacher Training College in Lincoln, UK. She spent several years in Nigeria - West Africa before the outbreak of the Biafran civil war teaching primary school aged children – initially from a sandpit.

She continued teaching English in the rebel state of Biafra during the war, following which she relocated to Birmingham, UK where she worked as a classroom teacher as well as co-authoring the first of many English text books for Macmillans publishers. These books became standard primary English texts in many states in Nigeria and other West African nations. In the 1970s she returned to Nigeria with her young family to be a classroom teacher and deputy headmistress in Bauchi State where she continued to produce text books for Macmillans. Many ex-pupils have spontaneously contacted her to express gratitude for the advantage her lessons gave them in later life – specifically with respect to the effective use of English language.

The 1980s were spent back in Birmingham, UK teaching at the inner-city Arden Primary school and among predominantly Asian communities. In the 1990s Wendy left classroom teaching and has since been adopted by the Korean Community as an expert in English language development both for visiting Academics attached to the Universities and for their children who return to Korea with the advanced conversational skills not easily obtained from traditional textbooks or online resources.

Wendy has decided to publish some of her worksheets for the first time, to enhance the learning experience of anyone needing to improve their use of English and to benefit from her 50+ years in teaching.

Introduction

This book has been written for people who have a good knowledge of basic English but would like to extend their vocabulary. It is suitable for teenagers and also for older people interested in improving their spoken or written English. It will also be very useful for people for whom English is their second language.

The exercises are self-corrective, the answers are available after each sentence, under each sentence, at the side of the exercise, at the end of the exercise or on a sheet after the exercise.

The words or phrases can be inserted in the sentences on the page or, for writing practice, the complete sentences can be re written on paper. As the words are all listed, a dictionary is not essential but may be of use for some students who will enjoy looking up the words and reading longer explanations of their usage.

Wendy Ijioma July 2020

Exercise
1

Select the appropriate word from the table below to fill the gaps

1. I stared for ages at the <u>vivid</u> sunset, the colours were so bright and clear, it was beautiful.

2. The teacher is _____ telling them not to talk during the lesson, but unfortunately her words fall on deaf ears.

3. Stop _____ me. I'll do it when I'm ready.

4. We decorated the inside of the house last year. Now we must paint the _____.

5. 'We need a place in which to hold our meeting.' 'I think there's a _____ room along this corridor.'

6. This is my son's first year at university. I'm quite excited as he will soon be home on _____.

7. This juice is concentrated. You need to _____ it before you use it.

8. We went up the hills to watch the _____ sunrise this morning.

9. There were so many _____ in his work that he had to re-do the exercise.

10. We WILL win this battle. We will never _____.

11. We had a small fire here yesterday because my sister left the chip pan on the gas stove, but fortunately mum was able to _____ it by smothering the flames with a towel.

12. I have a number of flowers in my garden, in _____ colours, red, yellow, blue, pink and white.

13. If you need a bed for the night that hotel has a number of _____.

vacant	vacancies	spectacular	exterior
surrender	extinguish	various	
constantly	dilute	errors	vacation
glorious	vivid	pestering	

Select the appropriate word from the table below to fill the gaps

"And so," Prof. Greggs _____ at the end of his speech, "I think you would be well advised to go ahead with the plan."

"Would it be _____ for me to call on Friday?" asked the young man, politely.

After the 3 mile race the poor horse was sweating _____.

He shook the bottle _____ before opening it.

Mary stroked the cat _____.
"Now, Jane, concentrate on your work," snapped the teacher.
"I would if it were remotely interesting," _____ Jane to her friend.

"The better your qualifications, the better the _____ of getting   a good job", explained the lecturer.

You must be very _____ when crossing that narrow bridge, because it has no handrail.

We're going to have the ------------------------- of our house painted,   but we'll have to leave the _____ till next year.

She lives in the heart of the country in a _____ little old cottage.

They tried in vain to _____ the horse into the horse box.

"I've got a dreadful cough," complained the customer to the pharmacist,   "can you suggest a good _____ ?"

The little worm _____ as I put it in the jar.

quaint	interior	cautious
muttered	coax	vigorously
squirmed	profusely	convenient
prospect	fondly	exterior
remedy	concluded	

Select the appropriate equivalent word or words from the table below to fill the gaps

1. What's the <u>height</u> of this mountain?
    The   -- altitude --- of the mountain is 3000 metres.

2. The prisoner escaped. He **wasn't caught** for three weeks.
    He e _ _ _ _ _   _ _ _ _ _ _ _

3. He had worked for twenty four hours without a break and was
    overcome with **weariness.**
    He was _ _ _ _ _ _ _ _ _ .

4. Her mouth dropped open in **utter surprise.**
    She was t_ _ _ _ _ _   _ _ _ _ _ _.

5. Abid is a **strong and healthy**   little lad.
    He is a very r_ _ _ _ _   y _ _ _ _   _ _ _ .

6. Thank you for your **help which I couldn't have done without.**
    I'm so grateful for your i _ _ _ _ _ _ _ _ _   a _ _ _ _ _ _ _ _ _ _.

7. I left because **she disliked** me so much.
    Because of h _ _   a _ _ _ _ _ _ _ _.

8. Don't **waste** your money.
    Don't s _ _ _ _ _ _ _ _ your money.

9. The **cars, buses and lorries didn't move** for three hours.
    The t _ _ _ _ _ _ _ was s _ _ _ _ _ _ _ _ _ for three hours.

10. I must go to the book shop to get some **pens, pencils and rubbers** for
    school. I must go to the book shop for some s _ _ _ _ _ _ _ _ _.

11. The sea was **calm.**
    It was t _ _ _ _ _ _ _.

4

12. We **put out to sea** on a **stormy** night.
We began our v _ _ _ _ _ on a t _ _ _ _ _ _ _ _ _ _ night.

13. In Egypt I saw this **huge** statue of a pharaoh.
It was c _ _ _ _ _ _ _ .

14. Michael will **show** you **how to do it**.
Michael will d _ _ _ _ _ _ _ _ _ the t _ _ _ _ _ _ _ _ .

15. Fido is a very **fierce** dog.
He is really f _ _ _ _ _ _ _ _ .

16. This dog is **pure bred** – I'm going to **show** him for Crufts Dog show.
Rover is a p _ _ _ _ _ _ _ . I'm going to e _ _ _ _ him for Crufts Dog show.

17. This is a strange fruit, **I don't think you can eat it.**
I don't think this fruit is e _ _ _ _ _ _ .

18. When I looked in her fridge it was disgusting – everything was <u>rotten</u>.
The fruit was p _ _ _ _ _ .

altitude	edible	her	squander	totally amazed
animosity	enter	invaluable	stationary	traffic
assistance	evaded capture	pedigree	stationery	tranquil
colossal	exhausted	putrid	technique	voyage
demonstrate	ferocious	robust	tempestuous	young boy

Select the appropriate word from the table on the right to fill the gaps

After swimming wash your costume in warm water to prevent it from _____ because of the chlorine in the water .

That is not my correct postcode. That's why the delivery of the letter was _____.

Is this the _____way to fold a napkin?

I _____ remember telling you to not to do that.

She was in floods of tears, she was so _____ when her dog died.

It's a beautiful sunny day, let's _____ across these fields .

My teacher _____the importance of writing neatly in a test.

The house next to ours hasn't been _____ for the last six months.

Many insects, birds and even squirrels enjoy living in _____ trees.

The company which makes these clothes has an excellent _____.

Mrs. Whatsit is very old so she has a _____ to live with her.

He lost his father a year ago and he is still _____.

A lot of work has gone into _____that building to its former glory.

Please put all those tins in the _____.

The _____ is so large that a thousand people can travel on it. It's a huge cruise liner.

The gold finch is quite a _____bird but I have a pair in my garden.

The coal tit is quite a _____bird. At least four visit my bird table daily.

I'm going to _____ a complaint, that was a truly terrible journey.

I'm _____it's the right thing to do.

The thief was _____ of the crime and sent to prison.

box	a container
certain	have no doubt
common	ordinary
companion	a friend who stays with you
company	having someone with you
convicted	found guilty
convinced	am quite sure
correct	right
delayed	arrived later than expected
distinctly	clearly
grieving	feeling sad after someone has died
hollow	nothing inside it
lodge a	to make a… complaint
meander	walk slowly, going nowhere in particular
occupied	lived in
perishing	being destroyed
rare	not many of them
reputation	what people think of you or your business
restoring	make it as good as before
stressed	emphasised, said how important something is
upset	distressed / unhappy
vessel	ship

Exercise
2

Word Study

endeavour	We should _____ to do our best work at all times
endured	The poor woman _____ many years of hardship
impertinent	She is so _____. She is always making rash decisions on the spur of the moment and then frequently regrets them
impetuous	Don't be so _____ , you should be polite to older people
rear	The car had punctures in both the _____ wheels
rare	It was such a _____ bird that many people came to see it.
loggerheads	They are always at _____, I don't think they ever stop quarrelling
logs	Please bring in plenty of _____ to put on the fire.
indolent	He is so _____, even when he has a job, he never does a full day's work
eminent	We have a very _____ professor coming to open the new science block
deficiency	If you have an iron _____ you may well feel too tired to study hard
energetic	He is very _____, he never seems to feel tired
prohibited	The playing of ball games is _____ in many residential areas
permitted	You are _____ to play football in the park.
illuminates	The bright light _____ the whole room
lubricate	I frequently _____ my bike to keep it in good condition
hurrying	The children are _____ to get to school early.
loitering	That man has been _____ round our houses for three hours. I'm going to ring the police
surpassed	She has _____ all our expectations
surmounted	She has a difficult childhood but she _____ all her problems superbly and now is a very successful lawyer

Words to express Movement
Select the appropriate word.

Come on, Sarah, I'm in a hurry – don't _____ .

        dawdle   **hurry**   **trudge**

I don't like the look of that man – he's been _____ around here all morning.

        skipping   **walking**   **loitering**

It was a brilliant, sunny afternoon, We had plenty of time so we _____ happily through the wood.

        strolled   **loitered**   **rushed**

In the summer the cows can _____ wherever they like, over the grassland, but in the winter they have to be kept in the byre.

        jump   **trip**   **wander**

The angry headmaster _____ onto the stage to address the pupils.

        walked   **strode**   **strolled**

I watched the aeroplane _____ into the evening sky.

        dash   **land**   **soar**

The snake _____ across the grass towards the sleeping child.

        slithered   **zoomed**   **tramped**

'Look at those two boys _____ to school as if they have nothing to do all day!'

        sauntering   **hurrying**   **slipping**

I watched the butterfly _____ from flower to flower in search of nectar.

        rushing   **flitting**   **crawling**

When we go to the city centre my mum rushes from shop to shop but I love to _____ by the toy shop window and admire all the wonderful toys which are displayed.

        tramp   **linger**   **loiter**

We _____ the mountain in three hours, and ate our picnic at the summit.

        fled   **scaled**   **scrambled**

The terrified villagers had to _____ the advancing army.

        approach   **run**   **flee**

The young man _____ down the street in his new army uniform.

        sauntered   **marched**   **lingered**

The children _____up the steep bank to reach the blackberries.

        skipped   **scrambled**   **soared**

The little old lady _____along in her high heeled shoes.

        tottered   **strolled**   **stamped**

We _____ happily around the park until dusk.

        wandered   **tripped**   **trudged**

We were just _____along with not a care in the world.

        plodding   **sauntering**   **walking**

The ducks _____ across the road to the duck pond.

        flew   **slid**   **waddled**

She _____ because the paving stones were uneven.

        tripped   **plodded**   **jumped**

The water was up to our knees so we had to _____through the sea till we got to the buoy.

        wade   **paddle**   **swim**

Her slippers were too large for her so she _____ along as best she could.

        shuffled   **slipped**   **slid**

For nearly six months after breaking her ankle the lady _____.

        strode   **loitered**   **limped**

We love to _____ in the sea.

        wade   **limp**   **paddle**

I _____ on the uneven ground and nearly broke my arm.

        plodded   **tripped**   **soared**

It was cold and dark and we had had a long day so we _____ wearily home.

        trudged   **marched**   **scrambled**

The soldiers _____ smartly along the road.

        marched   **trudged**   **plodded**

The boys _____ to greet their aunt who had brought them presents.

        slid   **shuffled**   **ran**

He _____ across the road to catch the bus and got knocked down by a motorcycle.

        limped   **shuffled**   **dashed**

The children may play in the garden but please tell them not to _____ on the flowers.

        trip   **walk**   **trample**

The boys _____ round the corner after the dog and ran into their headmaster.

        plodded   **dashed**   **tramped**

'Oh! Sorry – I _____ on the cat's tail.

        trod   **trampled**   **slipped**

The horse _____ round the field.

        cantered   **slithered**   **shuffled**

The horses _____ along the racecourse.
         galloped   **scrambled**   **marched**

It was wet and I _____ and fell as I walked home from school.
        dashed   **slipped**   **tottered**

We _____ across the room because our mother had
fallen asleep and we didn't want to disturb her.
        ran   **tiptoed**   **trod**

My father _____ quickly along the path to the caravan site.
        fled   **ran**   **limped**

Don't _____ from this narrow path because there's a swamp
on either side.
        flee   **stray**   **walk**

The army, well armed and refreshed by a good night's sleep _____
rapidly towards their enemies.
        shuffled   **wandered**   **advanced**

The farmer _____ across the ploughed field.
        plodded   **trod**   **marched**

The herd of elephants _____ over the crops and destroyed them.
        plodded   **trampled**   **scrambled**

I had twisted my ankle badly and had to _____ off the playing field.
        stumble   **limp**   **loiter**

The little child _____ unsteadily across the room.
        limped   **tottered**   **ran**

Please don't _____ on the flowers.
        hop   **run**   **tread**

He _____ quickly up the ladder and repaired the roof.
scrambled   walked   climbed

I think his ideas are outlandish. This means I think _____
he has good ideas / his ideas are very strange / his ideas are not good

That picture is hideous. This means the picture is _____
extremely unattractive   pretty   old   valuable

Match with words or phrases of **similar** meaning		
beneath contempt		
		often happens
indulges her every whim		
		utterly despicable
occurs frequently		
		a commendable attempt
despicable action		
		a really vile thing to do
a praiseworthy effort		
		gives her everything she wants

Exercise
3

Words to express movement (choose the correct tense)

hurry / hurried	_____ up, we'll be late
dash/dashed	I need some milk – I must _____ to the shop very quickly.
rush/rushed	There's no need to _____, there's plenty of time
tear/tore	The boys _____round the corner and bumped into the head teacher
climb/climbed	Only the fittest mountaineers can _____ Mount Everest
scramble/ scrambled	Yesterday we _____ up the bank
stride/strode	The head master _____ furiously into the hall
march / marched	The soldiers _____ along this road last week
sweep / swept	Lady Barnett _____ graciously into the room and greeted her guests
trot / trotted	The horse _____ across the field
canter / cantered	We _____ on our horses and then galloped

gallop / galloped	Yesterday the horses _____ round the racecourse
advance /advanced	As the army _____ the civilians retreated
retreat / retreated	Realising they were facing defeat the army _____
flee / fled	The women and children _____ from the advancing army
flit / flitted	We knew our neighbours were up to no good and then, last night, they did a moon light _____ just before the police arrived to arrest them.
jog /jogging	We passed the club members _____along the road
plod /plodded	Farmer Giles _____across the ploughed field
trudge / trudged	After a long day we _____ wearily home in the rain
trample / trampled	Please don't _____ on the flowers
Tread / trod / trample / trampled	_____ carefully, there are lots of bulbs and little flowers the grass. Try not to _____on them

Select the correct word to fill the gap from the table to the right

1. The castle is more than a thousand years old. It's a very _____ building.

2. This building was erected in the year 2020. It's very _____.

3. During the war people were restricted to very _____ rations – just enough food to keep them in good health, and no one wasted food, it was so precious.

4. It was a good year for fruit. There was sufficient rain and lots of sun shine. We had an _____ supply of plums and apples from the trees in our garden.

5. Some people live on junk food. They have a very _____ diet. Junk food doesn't contain all that you need to grow and be healthy.

6. If you eat plenty of fruit and vegetables and eat meat or fish, cheese, beans and drink milk you will have a _____ diet and that will help you to be strong and healthy.

7. If you are _____ you will spend your money wisely and not waste it.

8. If you are a _____ you will quickly spend all the money you get.

9. If you are a _____ you will get plenty of money but you will not spend it either on yourself or on other people.

10. If you are _____ you will willingly share whatever you have.

11. After we had walked ten miles we felt completely _____ so we found a B and B and stayed there for the night. We felt _____ after a good night's sleep and completed the walk easily.

12. When there is a _____ the crops don't grow for lack of rain and there may be a _____. Then, the children will be hungry every day unless people in other countries where there is an _____ of food send some to them.

13. Sometimes it rains so hard that the water level in the river _____ so high that it overflows its banks and there is a _____. Water may even get into people's homes. They have to move upstairs or go and stay with relations or friends until the water _____.

14. Our P.E teacher is so _____ she makes us practise hard so that we can win all our matches. She wants us to do well and always encourages us.

15. James is very _____. He runs a mile before breakfast every day, swims every evening, climbs hills on Saturdays and spends two hours on the trampoline on Sundays.

16. Jane is so _____. She gets up late, she won't walk to school, her father takes her in the car, she always makes an excuse so that she doesn't have to do P.E and so she never has any exercise at all. She's not interested in doing anything _____.

17. When you buy bread it's _____ but if you leave it for a week it will be _____.

18. She dropped the vase. It _____ into many pieces and the _____ were scattered all over the floor.

19. There are six books in the series and I have got the _____ set.

20. The parcel I received was marked '_____' because it contained a glass vase which would break very easily.

spendthrift	generous	ancient	meagre
exhausted	thrifty	miser	modern
famine	flood	subsides	enthusiastic
stale	shattered	fragments	whole
fresh	rises	abundance	lethargic
refreshed	abundance	athletic	'Fragile Handle with care'
drought			flood

Select the correct word to fill the gap from the table on the right

Small aeroplanes can be kept in a _____

Bees are kept in a _____

In a zoo birds are kept all together _____

A large number of fish can be kept in an _____

Chickens are hatched in an _____

Premature babies are placed in an _____

Criminals are kept in a _____ or a _____

Fruit trees are grown in an _____

Grapes are grown in a _____

Historical relics are shown in a _____

Operations are performed in a _____

Plays are performed in a _____

People are buried in a _____

Soldiers are stationed in the _____

Water for a town is stored in a _____

Young plants are reared in a _____

Lose tea leaves can be kept in a _____

Food for a picnic is put in a _____ _____

Hot tea or coffee is kept in a _____ when you go on a picnic

The tired old professor _____ on and on.

"Help!" _____ the terrified child

"You'll never reach the starting post" _____ the vile man, who despised his adversary, confident that he was going to win

"I can't run any further," _____ the exhausted athlete

"I always win," _____ the over – confident teenager

flask	caddy	picnic basket	hive	nursery
aquarium	barracks	aviary	incubator	cemetery
museum	prison	vineyard	orchard	hangar
theatre	reservoir	incubator	theatre	jail (sometimes spelt gaol)
boasted	rambled	whimpered	gasped	replied

Exercise 4

Male And Female

The _____ and duchess walked slowly down the red carpet

I met the _____ who wrote Harry Potter

When we have a party at our house my mum is the hostess
and my dad is the _____

Princess Anne's older brother is Charles. She is Charles' _____

Before a lady is married she is a spinster
Before a man is married he is a _____

In Scotland a girl is called a _____,
and a boy is called a _____

My Mum has a sister who has a son and a daughter
They are my _____

If the king and queen have a daughter she will be a _____

A man who looks after sheep is a _____

A person who makes suits for men is a _____
and a person who makes clothes for a lady is a _____

A man who cuts men's hair is a _____
A lady who cuts hair is a _____

A man who acts in plays is an _____,
and a lady who acts in plays is an _____

A person who rides a horse in a race is a _____

When my mother and father got married my mother was his _____
and my father was her _____

Jane's parents have three children, two girls and one boy, so Jane has a
sister and a _____

His uncle and ------------------ are coming to stay for a fortnight

Carol and Jack have been married for five years.
They have a son and a _____

Look at the duck and _____ with their brood of ducklings

The goose and _____ were swimming with their six goslings

duke	host	lass	author	lad	bachelor
sister	cousins	tailor	shepherd	hairdresser	seamstress
actor	jockey	barber	brother	aunt	drake
gander	daughter	actress	princess	husband	wife

The wife of the king is the _____
      duchess   queen   lady

Male means _____ Female means _____
      a girl   a boy

A male horse is called a _____   A female horse is called a
_____
      mare   foal   stallion   pony

A baby horse is called a _____ A small horse is called a
_____
      foal   pony   mare   stallion

A lot of trees altogether is called a _____ or a _____
and a lot of fruit trees is called an _____
      orchard   forest   wood

The short way to write 'Doctor' when you are writing about Doctor
Smith is _____
      Doc. Smith   Dr. Smith   doctor Smith

If one person is singing alone she is singing a _____
      solo   duet

If two people are singing or playing a musical instrument together we
say they are singing or playing a _____
      solo   duet

If we are very cold we say we are 'as _____ as _____'
and that is called a _____
      ice   cold   simile

If the baby is good we might use a simile and say
'He / she is as _____ as _____
      rude   good   silver   gold

Look, your bag is _____, under the table.
      here   hear   hare

Please can you speak louder, I can't _____ you.
      here   hear   hare

Can you _____ the music?
      here   hear   hare

Put your books _____
    here   hear   hare

We have a saying : As mad as the Mad March _____
    here   hear   hare

It was March and the _____ ran and leaped across the field
    here   hear   hare

Where are you? Oh _____ you are.
    here   hear   hare

If you stumble it means that you _____
    nearly fall   break your leg   are lame

If an old man is shuffling to the door it means he is _____
    taking long strides   is lame   isn't picking up his feet

The boys _____ along the corridor and nearly knocked the head master over
    dawdled   dashed   hopped

The headmaster _____ angrily onto the stage
    strode   rode   skipped

James and John decided to have a midnight feast. They _____ downstairs and raided the fridge
    sauntered   crept   skipped

"Hurry up," shouted her mother, impatiently, "stop _____"
    dawdling   trampling   plodding

What is the correct name for the noise which these animals make?	
A snake _____	A lion _____
A sheep _____	A donkey _____
A horse _____	A wolf _____
howls neighs brays bleats roars hisses	

Tim doesn't open his mouth when he is speaking and he doesn't use his lips. He _____ his lines in assembly, and no one could hear him

      muttered   **uttered**   **mumbled**

Peter was angry. "Stupid man," he _____rudely, under his breath

      muttered   **mumbled**   **hissed**

He was _____ up and down the room, desperately anxious for news

      walking   **racing**   **pacing**

Name three joints in your body: _____ _____ _____

      arm   **elbow**   **hand**   **wrist**   **leg**   **knee**

What are good quality belts, handbags and shoes made from? _____

      plastic   **leather**   **silk**

Newly baked bread is described as _____ but bread which is week old would be called _____

      new   **fresh**   **stale**   **old**   **rotten**

Use the adjectives below to fill the gaps

At the sea side you may notice that the sea is _____or _____

An animal may be _____or _____

A glass is _____ but a dish is o_____

On a bike the handle bars are _____ but the brake wires are _____

Material for a party dress will be _____ but for curtains it will be _____

    flexible   **wild**   **opaque**   **fine**   **tame**   **calm**   **rigid**   **rough**   **coarse**
           transparent

How many are there in:			
a dozen		half a dozen	
a couple		a brace	
a score		a gross	
a ream of paper		a century	
a millennium		a decade	

144 ; 2 ; 10 ; 500 ; 6 ; 1,000 ; 100 ; 20 ; 12 ; 2

He was an _____ father, he gave her everything she wanted.

They held two _____ views. They never agreed.

The _____ in Rwanda led to many thousands of deaths.

The choir sang in _____.

Thank you for your _____ contribution to the charity.

That's an _____ idea, let's do it!

This patch of ground has been _____ for years. My grandfather was growing vegetables on it before I was born.

We can go into the wood, but we must not pick the _____ flowers.
I don't see her very often, she visits only _____.

conflict	harmony	generous
conflicting	cultivated	wild
indulgent	occasionally	admirable

Write in the **opposite** meaning of the word in black			
strict	_____	strife	_____
mean	_____	frequently	_____
harmony	_____	wild	_____
peace generous rarely tame lenient discord			

Exercise 5

Find the meaning of the underlined word from the table below

1. In England the <u>prevailing</u> wind is the west wind.

2. Railway lines are always <u>parallel.</u>

3. The British <u>climate</u> is warm in summer and quite cold in winter.

4. Whether or not he stole the chicken is <u>irrelevant</u> because he Is in prison for a much more serious crime.

5. Although the sky was <u>overcast,</u> it was warm enough for our picnic.

6. She became very religious and <u>renounced</u> all bad things.

7. He was so happy he felt he was riding on the <u>crest</u> of a wave.

8. She tried so hard to help him but her efforts were <u>in vain.</u>

9. The <u>peasants</u> <u>toiled</u> all day in the fields and had barely enough to eat.

10. In the past the <u>correct etiquette</u> was for a man to <u>doff</u> his cap to a lady when he met her in the street.

11. She tried hard to <u>ignite</u> the fire but the wood was <u>damp.</u>

12. The sky was so clear we could easily see the <u>constellation.</u>

13. Donkeys can carry heavy <u>burdens.</u>

most frequent	gave up	group of stars	right thing to do
light	lift / raise	the top	slightly wet
the same distance apart	usual weather conditions	not connected with the matter	poor farm workers
worked hard	were of no use	cloudy	loads

Select the appropriate word to fill the gap from the table below

In the city centre motorists are banned, the area is for p_____ only.

Everyone has heard of the Queen. She is one of the most f_____ people in the world.

If you do something wrong you may end up in p_____.

A country which is not your own country is a f_____ country.

At first Peter's job was only temporary, but after six months it was made p_____.

She likes to buy lots of clothes. She is very e _____.

I can't afford to buy that coat, it's too e_____.

She doesn't come to Birmingham often, so I s_____ see her.

This water isn't deep, in fact it's quite s _____

The water was up to my knees. I had to w_____ through the water to get the ball back.

You can see clearly through that window, the glass is t _____.

The glass in the door is t_____, it lets light through but you can't see clearly.

You can't see through the door at all. It's o_____.

Mr. and Mrs. Jones wanted to rent a house, so they went to a letting agency and they were shown a house which was v_____ so they were able to move in immediately.

We wanted to stay somewhere cheap for the night and we were so lucky to find a B and B with a sign at the window saying v_____.

This material isn't soft, it's rather c_____.

coarse	pedestrians	opaque	seldom
famous	wade	prison	vacant
vacancies	translucent	extravagant	transparent
permanent	expensive	foreign	shallow

Words Using the prefix 'un' = 'not'

1. The tired old man _____ slowly and went to bed.

2. I didn't like the school, the staff and the other pupils were so _____.

3. My future plans are _____ at the moment.

4. If you have an _____ lifestyle you cannot expect to live to a ripe old age.

5. The _____ policeman bravely tackled the violent criminal single handed.

6. The vertical lines on that book are of _____ length.

7. I was delighted to see the nuthatch in my garden yesterday, it's an _____ bird in this region.

8. Mrs. Smith told her son not to play with James, as she considers him an _____ person to be his friend.

9. Pauline is always by herself at playtime, she is the most _____ girl in the class.

10. I've helped you all I can but you've never thanked me. You are very _____ .

11. Uncle Jim never laughs much, my mum says it's because he had an _____ childhood.

12. Don't believe what you hear about her, all those stories are _____ .

13. If there are dark clouds in the sky it is _____ to out without an umbrella or a rain coat.

14. He has no qualifications, he's just an _____ workman.

15. Matthew was knocked down by a bus and was _____ in hospital for a week.

16. Yesterday we had some very _____ visitors. We all hate it when Uncle John and Auntie Mary come.

17. Sometimes the bus comes at 7:o'clock, sometimes it comes at ten past seven and sometimes it doesn't come till nearly half past seven. It's very _____.

18. She was discharged from hospital last week but she is still _____ on her feet.

19. She needs help because she is still very weak after her illness but her daughter is _____ to do anything for her.

20. You expect me to finish all that work today? It will take me at least 20 hours, you're being _____.

unsteady	unreasonable	ungrateful	unhappy
unfriendly	unequal	uncommon	unwelcome
unskilled	unconscious	unreliable	unwilling
unsuitable	undressed	uncertain	unarmed
unhealthy	unpopular	untrue	unwise

The farmers in Egypt are able to grow crops because of the _____ which is a kind of mud (wet soil) brought down the River Nile.

      earth   **silt**   **rubbish**

Every ten years in the United Kingdom there is a _____ to find out how many people are in the country.

      election   **census**   **decade**

I'm sure their plans will _____ because they lack the necessary expertise to make them work.

      succeed   **crash**   **founder**

The pendulum on the old grandfather clock _____ to and fro all the time.

      flashed   **rang**   **swung**

Seeds remain _____ during the winter and then come to life in the spring.

      sleeping   **quiet**   **dormant**

She was the _____ of our local museum for many years.

      curator   **keeper**   **matron**

I think the _____ of seeds is quite remarkable – every different kind of plant has its own way of getting its seeds away from the parent plant.

      dispersal   **distribution**   **scattering**

He doesn't drink alcohol. He has always been _____.

      drunk   **sober**   **tea-total**

It's a _____ing thought that many drivers whom you pass late at night may well be the worse for drink or drugs.

      frightening   **funny**   **interesting**

The age at which you can drive a car in England is _____.

      16   **17**   **18**

The number of stars in the sky is in_____.

      large   **many**   **infinite**

You're a disgrace! Your mother would _____ your behaviour.

      enjoy   **deplore**   **disagree**

That chair is priceless. This means

It's worthless / it's valuable / it is so valuable it is not possible to put a price on it

I fear her condition will _____ over the next few weeks.
      improve   **fail**   **deteriorate**

He seems to _____ between deciding to stay or deciding to go.
      be unsure   **change**   **vacillate**

If we are going to succeed we need a _____ of opinion.
      consensus   **agreement**   **joining**

I enjoy his sense of _____, it amuses me.
      nonsense   **stupidity**   **humour**

If you don't _____ with the rules you will be fined.
      comply   **agree**   **break**

It was a very rare animal so when it died the zoo keeper sent the body to
a _____ to have it stuffed and put in a museum.
      tannery   **hairdresser**   **taxidermist**

As the floods _____ the occupants of the affected houses returned to
take stock of the situation.
      deteriorated   **rose**   **receded**

What's the difference between a jerkin, a gherkin and a Gurkha ?
   a)   a small pickled cucumber
   b)   a soldier from Nepal (a country near India) who joined the British army
   c)   a kind of short jacket
         a jerkin is _____
         a gherkin is _____
         a Gurkha is_____

What is a geyser? _____
a natural fountain of hot water   an old man   a kind of mountain

What is an old geezer? _____
      an old man   **an old spring of water**   **an old mountain**

Exercise
6

1. Please, mum, stop _____ me.

2. There was a slight _____ this morning but it soon cleared and then the day was bright.

3. The voice of the teacher droned on _____.

4. It's not good to travel in Bangladesh at that time, it will be the middle of the _____ season.

5. He made a _____ mistake.

6. She was born with a cleft _____.

7. The little chick lay in the _____ of my hand.

8. The artist mixed his paint on his _____.

9. No one has ever seen a _____ because it's an extinct flying reptile.

10. I will not allow such behaviour. I shall give him a severe _____.

11. You must put it in _____ the right place. A millimetre either way would be disastrous.

12. We planted the _____ in the front garden.

13. Well, I'll try to _____ the courage to face him.

14. This bedroom smells _____, let's open the windows.

monsoon	musty	muster	sapling	mist
pterodactyl	palate	monotonously	mollycoddling	exactly
palette	reprimand	monumental	palm	

Replace the underlined words from the list on the right	
He arrived on time	
	a mane
The stallion had hair on his neck which was long and black	
	at dusk
The two baby sheep gambolled around their mother	
	bad odour
You have two options	
	choices
The sailor was happy to be going to sea again	
	concealed
We shall leave as the sun sets	
	damp
There's a nasty smell coming from those pipes	
	forbidden
I like to ramble across the countryside	
	frolicked
I hid the treasure in the loft	
	lambs
In America the roads are broader than in England	
	male horse
Balls games are prohibited on this grass	
	mariner
The stallion reared and bucked and no one could ride him	
	punctually
To clean the table I used a slightly wet cloth	
	roam

43

Select the correct word from the table opposite to fill the gap

1. Because of the gr _ _ _ ty of the problem they decided to refer the matter to the committee.

2. The deranged man was so un _ _ _ _ ictab _ _ , one minute he was sweet and calm and the next he was shouting and screaming like a mad man.

3. No one wants to buy this house because of its _ _ o _ _ _ ity to the airport, which is why the present owners wish to move; they are disturbed up to twenty times a day by planes taking off or landing.

4. If you look up into the night sky you can sometimes see many cl _ _ _ _ _ _ of stars. It was stars which used to guide travellers before modern instruments like the compass and nowadays the GPS.

5. Donkeys are useful, for they can carry heavy l _ _ _ _ _ .

6. If you e _ _ _ _ _ the speed limit along this road you are likely to incur a £70 fine.

7. The Boy Scouts tried in vain to ex _ _ _ _ _ _ _ _ _ the fire.

8. It was an uncomfortable meeting because of the ho _ _ _ le relationship between the two groups of people. They couldn't agree about anything.

9. He told his son, "you mustn't cross the road u _ _ _ _ _ _ an adult is with you."

10. It's es _ _ _ _ _ _ _ _ that we make the decision now. If we don't the whole plan will fall through.

11. It will be up to you to make the f _ _ a _ decision.

12. The weather has been quite m _ _ _ of late.

	Definitions
clusters	groups
essential	absolutely necessary
exceed	on a road – to go faster than the law permits
extinguish	put out a fire
final	last (after that no further discussion)
gravity	seriousness
hostile	unfriendly
innocent	not guilty, he / she has not done anything wrong
loads	a heavy weight to be carried somewhere
mild	referring to the weather – not too cold, not hot
polite	doing what is right, keeping the traditions
proximity	nearness
the judge	When a person has been convicted of a crime it is the judge who decides what the punishment should be
unless	except – but if something else is ...then you can
unpredictable	Not knowing what he will do next

13. She has a terrible _ _ _den to bear. Not only does she have a full time job and three small children, she also has a sick husband and an aged mother.

14. He did so well, he   _ _ _pas_ _ _ all our expectations.

15. Our neighbourhood is quite a _ f_ _ _ _ _ _ nearly every person is working and most have professional jobs.

16. The flowers looked so natural but in fact they were _ _ ti _ _ _ ial

17. That family lives in p _ _ _ _ ty, they have barely enough to eat.

18. The old lady who lives in that ramshackle old house is so _ _ _ er _ _ _ _ , she has very little money yet she is always giving money to help other   people.

19. My friend is very _ _ pu_ _ _, everyone likes her.

20. Last night an _ _tru _ _ _ broke the window and entered our house but we heard the thief and we called the police.

21. My sister is so   _ lu_ _ y, yesterday I asked her to carry a pot of flowers into the garden and she dropped it.

22. My u_ _ _ _ and his wife live not far from our house.

23. My four   _ous_ _ will come to stay with me during the summer holiday.

24. Tomorrow is a very special day for us, we are having a big party in our garden. We are concerned about the weather. Rain will destroy all our plans of having a _ar _ _ _ _ _ _. I think it will rain. I'm a pes_ _ _ _ _ _ but my sister is an op_ _ _ _ _ and thinks it will be fine ! I hope she is right.

25. My mother's sister is my _ _ _ _ _

Definitions

affluent	having a lot of money – well off financially
artificial	not real, it may refer to flowers not grown in a garden, or made in a factory or hand made by a skilled craftsman or craftswoman
aunt / auntie	your mother or father's sister
barbecue	a meal grilled, cooked outside and eaten out side
burden	a very heavy load / a heavy mental load
clumsy	lacking physical coordination – often dropping things
cousins	the children of your mother or father's brothers or sisters
generous	sharing what you have with other people even if you haven't got much yourself.
intruder	a person who breaks into someone's house
optimist	someone who thinks the best will happen
pessimist	someone who thinks the worst will happen
popular	liked by everyone
poverty	not enough money to live on
surpassed	did better than expected
uncle	your mother or father's brother

Select the correct word to fill the gap from the list on the right

The witch filled her _____ with slugs, spiders and worms.	calm
Soldiers must stand _____ when they salute the Queen.	cauldron
Mary was looking through the _____ in her cabin on the liner.	erect
I bought a _____ melon this morning.	honeydew
In hot weather I always have my lunch on the _____	launched
The moon waxes and _____ every month.	managed
We _____ a coin to see who should go first.	meagre
The men finished building the boat on Tuesday and it was _____ on Thursday.	obstinate
We had a lot of visitors last week and mum said she couldn't have _____ without my help.	patio
The sea was so _____ we just floated lazily in it all day.	porthole
We couldn't swim in the _____ sea	rough
That donkey is so _____ . If it doesn't want to move you just can't make it go.	scantily
I don't like visiting my aunt, she always gives us such _____ portions of food.	tossed
She must have been cold, she was so _____ dressed.	wanes

Write sentences to show the difference between:

road _____

_____

_____

rode _____

_____

_____

rowed_____

_____

_____

Exercise 7

Select the correct word from the column on the right

Words which mean '2'

I'll be ready in a _____ of minutes.

I have three p_____ of shoes.

I rang your door bell t_____ but there was no answer.

Last year we raised £100 for charity and this year we want to _____ that amount.

Our house has _____ glazing.

First she had triplets then she had _____.

The _____ carried all our baggage up the mountain for us.

A pedestrian is a person who is _____ .

To shiver means _____ .

Because Jake was not well the party was _____ for a week.

The child has a _____ so she will have an operation on her eye when she is a little older.

twins
_____

double
_____

twice
_____

pair = two the same
_____

couple
_____

pedestrian = a person who is walking
_____

postponed = to put off for a while
_____

shiver = to shake with cold
_____

squint = to look in different directions with each eye
_____

mule = an animal which is used to carry baggage or people up steep pathways.

A mule is a cross – breed the mother is a horse and the father is a   donkey

Harry: 'You're so beautiful.'
Mary: 'You're _____ me! I'm not beautiful!'

The men with the bulldozer _____ the building
and the builders have started to _____ a new one.

It is _____ to board a train without buying
a ticket.

Riding bicycles is _____ here.

We were thrilled that the _____
musician was to give a concert in Symphony Hall. We
have already bought tickets to go to it.

When the captain shouted "_____ ship" everyone
on board rushed to the side and jumped overboard.
The ship was sinking.

The foolish couple who won the lottery _____
their winnings.

What is your favourite _____? I prefer tea to
coffee.

abandon =
leave, get out of
_____

beverage =
any drink except
water
_____

demolished =
pulled down
_____

eminent =
famous
_____

erect =
to build
_____

flattering =
praising someone
more than they
_____

illegal =
against the law
_____

prohibited =
forbidden
_____

squandered =
wasted their money

Replace the words underlined with a word from the table on the right

1. We **walked slowly** over the ploughed fields.

_ _ _ _ _ _ _ _ _

2. I **noticed** you looked extremely tired this morning. What's wrong?

_ _ _ _ _ _ _ _ _

3. The **price for** parking your car there is **exorbitant!**

_ _ _ _ _ _ _ _ _   _ _ _ _ _ _ _ _ _

4. She's so **hard working,** we all admire her.

_ _ _ _ _ _ _ _ _

5. If you **stop me from working** any longer we shall miss the bus.

_ _ _ _ _ _ _ _ _

6. The **tramp** came to my door and asked for a sandwich and a cup of tea.

_ _ _ _ _ _ _ _ _

7. She is **very sad** because her husband has **left** her.

_ _ _ _ _ _ _ _ _   _ _ _ _ _ _ _ _ _

8. I'm so **happy** to see you.

_ _ _ _ _ _ _ _ _

9. Don't worry, it's **not important.**

_ _ _ _ _ _ _ _ _

10. Stop **annoying** me!

_ _ _ _ _ _ _ _ _

11. The plane should **leave** at 9:30

_ _ _ _ _ _ _ _ _

12. We **walked slowly** and happily through the wood, going nowhere
    in particular.   _ _ _ _ _ _ _ _ _

vagabond / vagrant	pleased / delighted/ glad	observed / perceived	thrilled / delighted	irritating / pestering
hinder me / delay me	trivial / Insignificant	not reasonable / excessive	industrious / diligent	abandoned
wandered	depart / go	distraught / upset/ distressed	tramped / plodded	cost of/ fee

Words with the prefix 'Dis'

Jane had to use a wheel chair because she's _____.

The teacher told the boys not to go into the hall. Peter and Joe were _____ They went into the hall and got caught by the head teacher so they're in trouble.

When the plumber came to replace our old gas boiler he had to_____ the gas for three hours.

You think that there are wild ostriches living in Scotland? I _____.
You're wrong. Wild ostriches only live in Africa.

I would like to play basket ball but I'm not very tall. It's a _____ to be short if you want to play basket ball.

I think that Anna is a very _____ girl. She never smiles and she always argues with everyone.

My mother doesn't know that I play with Simon. She would _____ so I daren't tell her. She doesn't think he is a suitable friend for me!

The burglar had a gun but the brave policeman walked up to him and _____ him.

A burglar broke into our house so when we returned from our holiday my room was in _____. The thief was looking for money. It took me all day to tidy it.

After my operation I suffered some _____ but I wasn't in pain.

I wanted to replace the plate I broke but that line has been _____ so I couldn't get one to match.

The book cost £12 but they gave us a £2 _____ so we only had to pay £10.

We often play in that _____ factory. No one ever comes near it but the door is wide open.

My favourite season is summer. I _____ the cold but I love the hot weather.

I wanted to enter the competition but my teacher _____ me. He said I wasn't good enough to enter.

disabled   **disapprove**   **disagreeable**   **discount**   **dislike**

disadvantage   **disagree**   **discomfort**   **discontinued**   **discouraged**

disconnect   **disarmed**   **disarray**   **disused**   **disobedient**

If you are physically disabled you may have to use a _____ to get around.

What do you dislike most? _____

Is your bedroom usually tidy or constantly in disarray? _____

If a shop advertised a discount on an item will you pay more or less for it? _____

Would it be an advantage or a disadvantage to be clever? _____

If you're discourteous does it mean you're polite or rude? _____

Exercise
8

Select another word for :

soar		fetch		serious
depart		enjoy		trivial
arrive		delighted		
vagabond		comprehend		

tramp	rise up	Like very much	leave	unimportant
retrieve	grave	understand	very pleased	come

Select the appropriate word from the table above to complete the sentences below

My dog will _____ the ball when I throw it.

At the airport I like to watch the planes _____ into the sky.

The _____ looked hungry so I gave him a sandwich.

Did you _____ the concert?

The plane from France will _____ at 6 o'clock.

I can't _____ this book.

This is only a _____ problem, it's not serious.

We expect our visitors to _____ this afternoon.

I'm _____ to tell you that you passed the exam.

We've left the dog's lead is at granny's, can you run and _____ it for me, please.

This is a very _____ matter. We must call meeting at once to discuss it.

My dog runs and _____ the ball whenever I throw it for him.

General Knowledge

1.   What is a bugle? _____

2.   What does a door need to make it possible to swing it open and shut? _____

3.   A pike is a kind of fresh water _____

4.   Bream and roach live in _____ and _____

5.   Herring and mackerel are kinds of _____ _____ _____

6.   There was a large _____ in church this morning

7.   A period of 10 years is a _____

8.   A hundred years is a _____ A thousand years is a _____

9.   A lot of herring swimming together is called a _____ of herring

10. At the concert Stephen sang all by himself. He sang a _____

11. Thomas and Philip Smith are _____. Thomas is 5 minutes older than his brother

12. A squirrel's home in a tree is called a _____

13. A female fox is a _____

14. Asia, Europe, Africa, America and Oceania are all _____

15. If you are lost at sea you will need a _____ to show you the right direction

16. Name 8 points on the compass
     _____ _____
     _____ _____
     _____ _____
     _____ _____

compass	north west	drey	twins
century	rivers and lakes	fish	hinges
congregation	salt water fish	south	solo
continents	south east	north	decade
millennium	a musical instrument like a trumpet	vixen	shoal
north east	south west	west	east

61

Which month comes after July? _____

Which month comes before November? _____

What relation is your <u>sister</u> to your <u>father</u>? She is his _____

What is a <u>B & B</u> ? _____

If a B&B has <u>vacancies</u> what does it mean? _____

If product A is of **'<u>superior quality</u>'** to Product B – will it be better or worse?   _____
In which case   Product B will be of _____   quality.

Some snakes are harmless, but some can kill you because they are _____

Mrs. Smith is lenient, but Mrs. Jones is the opposite. She is very _____

The sheep got out through a hole in the fence. What is another word for a 'hole'? _____

<u>Collective nouns</u>

All the teachers in a school make up the _____

All the sailors on a ship make up the _____

All the people watching a football match are the _____

All the people at a concert or at the theatre are the _____

All the people at a church service make up the _____

A group of people singing together will form a _____

audience	gap	staff
August	inferior	strict
better	Bed and Breakfast = a room in a private house where you can stay	inferior
choir		spectators
congregation	daughter	there is an unoccupied room for you to stay in
crew	October	venomous

After running 8 kilometres before breakfast I returned home _____ .

You must have worked very hard, I'm _____ at your progress.

That's the second glass you've dropped today; you're so _____ .

I feel rather _____ , I think I'll go to bed for a while.

It's a wet day, her mother has gone to town and the TV is broken. She feels _____ .

My uncle is a _____ man; he's always laughing and playing jokes on us.

Jessica is OK now, after her shock, but she's still a bit _____ .

Miss. Jones was amazing. Even when the shelf fell on her while we were getting ready for the performance, she was quite _____ . She just pushed it upright and called the carpenter to fix it. Then she continued the rehearsal as if nothing unusual had happened.

Peter doesn't like talking about his time in prison. When John mentioned it there was an _____ silence.

The teacher was _____ when we arrived late, but my parents were even more _____ when they were told about it because they had sent us to school in plenty of time.

amazed = surprised

annoyed = cross, angry,

awkward = clumsy, difficult to deal with, embarrassing

bored = having nothing to do

clumsy = not agile; always dropping things

drowsy = sleepy

famished = starving, very, very hungry

furious = very very angry

jovial = jolly, merry, always laughing

tearful = nearly crying

unruffled = not easily upset

Harder Words

1. I felt upset because the head master _____ my ideas.

    She _____ the priceless pearls in the loft so that no one could steal them.

    You _____ me. You told me you were going to stay with your friend, but you went to a night club instead.

    He is so _____ and so thoughtful and polite as well as hard working, he deserves to succeed.

    My oldest known ancestor was born _____ 1378.

    <u>concealed</u>   <u>courteous</u>   <u>deceived</u>   <u>derided</u>   <u>circa</u>

2. I feel rather _____ I think I'll retire early.

    Now, let me _____ the use of this wonderful machine.

    The evil man _____ capture for a decade.

    These fruits are _____ but you can't eat the ones in the box, they are inedible.

    I _____ any one who cannot stand up for what they believe.

    <u>demonstrate</u>   <u>despise</u>   <u>drowsy</u>   <u>edible</u>   <u>eluded</u>

3. We had an _____ crop of plums last year.

    She's so _____ , she thinks she's better than all of us and she won't listen to advice from any one.

    James is sure he saw an _____ last night but no one believes him, they don't believe in ghosts.

    Thank you for helping me in my time of _____ .

    He is very foolish. He ran up _____ bills which will take years to pay off.

    Mr. Jones used to be a nice man, but his success has made him unduly _____ nowadays he cares about nothing except making more money.

    <u>abundant</u>   <u>adversity</u>   <u>arrogant</u>   <u>apparition</u>   <u>avaricious</u>   <u>colossal</u>

1. The inhabitants of the village fled when they were warned that a hurricane was _____ .

2. I hear that Professor Jakes, the _____ professor of Physics, will speak at our _____ General Meeting.

3. If the annual rainfall in this country continues to _____ we shall not only face hose pipe bans, but also a rationing of the water required for daily use in the home.

4. That man has been _____ outside our house for three hours. I'm going to call the police, I'm sure he's up to no good.

5. The seemingly _____ army was overcome because their enemies used exceptionally clever _____ .

6. The female eagle always flies back to her _____ in the _____ at _____ .

7. The older sister is of normal height, but the younger is of _____ stature.

8. I have spent a lot of money making these replicas, but I hope to make a good _____ when I sell them.

9. The _____ foretold the catastrophe which we now face.

10. We were beset by a _____ of unruly youths.

11. In times of scarcity we all tend to _____ essential items.

12. What's your favourite _____ ? Mine is hot chocolate.

annual	beverage	brood	diminutive
eminent	eyrie	hoard	horde
prophet	profit	tactics	loitering
imminent	dusk	invincible	dwindle

Exercise 9

Select the correct word from the table to the right to fill the gap

1. There must have been at least a hundred fish in the _____ .

2. My father nearly bought a _____ in the south of France because he has always wanted to grow grapes and make his own wine.

3. The soldiers were confined to _____ because no one knew who the culprit was.

4. The cargo of televisions from Korea were put into the _____ of the ship, to be transported to England.

5. At the _____ we saw the shoes worn by children three hundred years ago and clothes worn by the Pharaoh (king) of Egypt long ago.

6. Crude oil (the oil which miners have got out of the ground) is cleaned and purified at a _____ .

7. If you are rich enough to own a private plane you will need a _____ to keep it in.

8. When we visited the zoo we saw a large number of rare birds in the _____ .

9. I love to go into our _____ in September and eat lots of juicy apples.

10. After writing my first novel I sent it to a publisher and the _____ made some corrections, then it was published.

11. When I play my violin in a _____ I watch the _____ throughout the _____ .

12. In 1947 my father bought all 23 volumes of the _____ Britannica so we could look up information on any subject. Now we use the internet instead.

	Definition
aquarium	a large tank for fish
aviary	like a large cage for birds
barracks	where soldiers live
concert	where musicians play their music to an audience
conductor	the person who stands at the front of an orchestra and directs the players with his baton
editor	a person who corrects manuscripts before they are printed
encyclopaedia	a book of information arranged in alphabetical order. There was a very famous series of 23 volumes (books) of information called the Encyclopaedia Britannica but now most people use the internet and Wikipedia to find out information.
hangar	a place to keep planes
hold	the bottom part of a ship where anything which is to be transported to another country is stored
museum	where old artefacts (objects) are kept to show us how ancient people lived
orchard	a place where fruit trees are grown
performance	when a group of people play music or act a play for an audience
refinery	where the oil which has brought out of the ground is cleaned
vineyard	where grapes are grown

Write one word or phrase to replace the underlined words

This vase is _worth a lot of money,_ but this one
is _priceless_ because
there is no other one like it in the whole world .

That man is _very well known._

I can't find the _way in._

Is this the _way out?_

Look! There's _P.C_ Bloggs walking down the street.

We walked from the mountain top to the
low lying land between the two mountains.

When we went on holiday we were diving in the sea and
we found _the ship which had sunk_ two _hundred years_ ago.
It was completely _covered with water._

It's _quite a cold day._

We had a meal at a very nice restaurant. After the
main course we had a delicious _pudding._

When we had finished eating we paid the bill
and the cashier gave my father the
paper on which it showed how much we had paid.

All the milk in this country is _boiled and then cooled_ to
kill any bad bacteria from the cattle.

He hurt his leg so he was _walking with uneven steps._

I forgot to water the flowers so they looked very _limp._

Be careful! That broken glass has a _rough, uneven_ edge.

We chose a good place to _put up_ our tent.

entrance	famous	dessert	droopy	wreck
pasteurised	erect	receipt	jagged	valuable
valley	limping	the Police Constable	chilly	centuries
discovered	exit	it is unique	submerged	invaluable

Birds begin to sing at dusk.   _____

It wasn't true. The story was a trick.   _____

She died of a strange disease.   _____

The sailor had sailed the seven seas.   _____

He was starving. He was given only very small helping of
food each day.   _____

It was difficult to persuade the horse to
enter the horse box.   _____

He's so agile he can climb up the highest tree.   _____

We like to have holidays on far away islands because we   _____
appreciate the peacefulness of these places.   _____

The smell from the drains was dreadful.   _____

The child was so rude that he was suspended from school.   _____

Playing ball on this estate is forbidden.   _____

She's very ill and nobody can find a cure.   _____

We are looking for a house in this
neighbourhood.   _____

We set off when the sun rose.   _____

odour	hoax	meagre	nimble /supple	remote
mariner	at dawn	twilight / sun set	malady	vicinity /area
coax	insolent	remedy	prohibited	tranquillity

What's Wrong???????

The underlined word is *wrong*, it's the opposite of the correct word. Find the correct word in the list to the right

The <u>audience</u> cheered at the end of the football match.

This <u>ancient</u> house was built just last year.

If you travel south for a long time you will eventually reach the <u>North Pole.</u>

The kangaroo is a <u>rodent</u> which lives in Australia.

The rat is a <u>marsupial</u> which lives underground.

Our new house is <u>vacant</u> so we can't move in yet.

We looked at the sign outside the B and B and it said '<u>No Vacancies</u>', so we went in and asked if we could have a room for the night.

We <u>strolled</u> as fast as possible along the city streets.

They <u>trudged</u> fast _and quickly got to the bus stop in time.

I had some <u>serials</u> for my breakfast.

The <u>wolves</u> pulled the sledge across the frozen wastes of the Arctic.

The student was delighted because she obtained <u>minimum</u> marks.

We got up early and listened to the bird song at <u>dusk.</u>

We could see clearly through the <u>opaque</u> glass.

No one has ever heard of this <u>famous</u> artist.

We wanted to <u>purchase</u> that valuable painting so we were delighted when the American lady put in an offer to buy it.

He's an excellent pupil, so industrious and <u>insolent.</u>

The <u>spectators</u> enjoyed the concert.

This <u>modern</u> building is more than a thousand years old,

a serial	a play on the radio or television which is divided into parts and broadcast in instalments over a period of several days or weeks
ancient	old
audience	people listening - to a concert or play
cereals	crops such as wheat or oats which are made into breakfast foods
dawn	early morning, the sun is rising
delighted	pleased
disappointed	not pleased
dusk	when light is fading and it's nearly dark, the sun is setting
famous	everyone knows the person
hurried	walked fast
huskies	dogs which have been trained to pull sledges across the snow
industrious	hard working
insolent	rude
marsupial	animal which carries its baby in its pouch
maximum	the most
minimum	the fewest
modern	new
obscure	unknown
occupied	someone is living in the house (or someone is in the room)
opaque	you can't see through it
polite	well behaved, someone who speaks nicely
ran	went very fast
rodent	mammal which gnaws its food
spectators	people watching - a football match or other sports
strolled	walked slowly in no particular direction
the north pole	in the far north, the south pole is in the far south of the world
to purchase	to buy
to saunter	to walk slowly and happily
to sell	to give someone something for money
transparent	you can see through it
trudged	walked slowly, heavily, not happily
upset	not happy
vacancies	there are empty rooms in the hotel / there are job opportunities
vacant	empty
wolves	wild animals rather like dogs

Exercise
10

Select the correct word from the table to the right to fill the spaces

1. We had to _____ ship when it began to sink.

2. At the end of the performance everyone _____

3. He loves writing the music for new songs. He's very good at _____ .

4. He came towards me _____ a weapon.

5. If you _____ with the rules you won't get into trouble.

6. We know you did it. If you _____ now you will not be in too much trouble.

7. Maria only speaks Polish. No one here speaks Polish so we shall have to ask her sister to come and _____ for her.

8. He speaks French fluently. He has _____ several books from French into English.

9. If you order online the parcel with be _____ to your door within a week.

10. The dogs were growling and _____ their teeth at each other.

11. The old building next to our house will soon be _____ to make room for some new houses.

12. This squash is concentrated. You need to _____ it with water before you drink it.

13. This is the right time of year to begin to _____ your garden.

14. The weather _____ is not good for the next weekend.

15. "Why do you need to put oil in your car?"
    "Because it _____ the engine."

16. When I was ill I went to the doctor's _____ and he gave me a prescription

17. I took the prescription to the _____ who gave me the medicine.

abandon	confess	forecast
applauded	cultivate	gnashing
brandishing		interpret
chemist / pharmacist	delivered	lubricates
composing	demolished	surgery
comply	dilute	translated

Her mother was in a hurry but Suzy _____ in front of the toy shop thinking wistfully how wonderful it would be if she could possess that beautiful doll.

The _____ travelled far and wide, buying exotic things at a cheap price with a view to selling them at a good profit back home.

She is so loyal to her friend who is not well, she is _____ by her bedside and seeing to her every need.

His mother tells him _____ not to do that but he doesn't listen to her.

Many _____ have come and gone. Once upon a time Britain was a great empire, controlling or ruling many countries.

The speed _____ in towns and built up areas is 30 mph but on the motorways it is 70mph.

Public means for the people - for everyone. In shopping centres and also in large shops There are _____ conveniences - which are toilets which anyone can use.

Last night they went to a _____ _____ for a drink.

As our army _____ the enemy _____ and we _____ So we won the battle.

Don't make a _____ decision, you may regret it, think carefully before you decide.

Many countries have a large _____ of ships ready to protect their country if the people from another country tries to invade .

Many organisations are working hard to _____ poverty from the world.

Definitions

a pub	short for 'a public house' - a place where any adult can go to buy a drink
advanced	went forward (often when talking about an army)
banish	to get rid of something bad.
constantly	frequently – nearly all the time
defeated	beaten in battle
empires	countries conquered and ruled by the most powerful country
fleet	a collective noun meaning a lot of ships belonging together, for example all the warships belonging to one country
frequently	many times
hasty	quick, acting without thinking
limit	an amount you must not exceed: a) There is a limit to how homework you should be expected to do in one evening; b) There's a speed limit to how fast cars are legally allowed to go.
lingered	was reluctant to move on. Wanted to stay there for a while.
merchant	someone who travels long distances to buy things which he can then sell at home and make a lot of money
public	all the people, open to everyone. A public meeting = anyone can go to it. A public toilet – is for everyone.
retreated	went back (often when talking about an army)

Select the correct word from the table below

1. What is the name of a female horse? _____

2. Name two kinds of berries which we can eat. _____

3. What do we fix on a door so that it can swing open and shut? _____

4. What do you press when you are driving a car to make it stop? _____

5. What do you press when driving a car to make it go faster? _____

6. Name a musical instrument that is like a bugle. _____

7. What musical instrument do the Scottish people like to play? _____

8. When you are building a house what do you put between layers of bricks to stick the bricks together? _____

10. What is the name of a male pig?   _____
                                          a female pig?   _____
                                          a baby pig?   _____

11. What is a herring?   _____

12. What do we call a smoked, dried herring?   _____

13. What two things do British business men carry to work? One is to protect them from the rain and the other is to hold the work they had to do at home in the evening. _____   _____

14. In a shop or a restaurant, etc. where can large sums of money be kept safe? _____

15. Name a precious stone. _____

16. What word means 'old' when referring to castles? _____

ancient	a fish	a sow	bagpipes	accelerator
diamond	a kipper	a piglet	trumpet	raspberries
ruby	an umbrella and a brief case	mortar (=a mixture of cement, sand and water)	mare	blackberries
a safe	a boar	brake	hinge	gooseberries

Select one word from the table below for each of the following

go into		go up	
go back		go down	
go forward		go away	
go away in a hurry		go well	
go on		go towards	

advance	ascend	descend	flee	leave
approach	continue	enter	flourish	retreat

The missing words below are all verbs and are all in the past tense

1. The army had_____ because the enemy was attacking ferociously.

2. The other army which was better equipped _____ with confidence.

3. I was watching the cat as it _____ the bird.

4. Don't stop, you haven't _____ your work.

5. He was so miserable that he _____ into the depth of depression.

6. The police _____ the derelict house at midnight but the thieves had _____ with the loot.

7. We _____ wearily home in the pouring rain.

8. The farmer _____ across the ploughed field.

9. We _____ the king's palace in fear and trepidation.

entered	sank	retreated	fled	plodded
advanced	finished	trudged	chased	approached

81

Vocabulary - Find a word in the table to the right which means nearly the same as the word or words in brackets

1. Although he says it was not his fault, I still think he's (guilty) _____.

2. Make sure that door is locked (well) _____ before you leave.

3. Don't drink that water until you have boiled it, it's (not clean) _____.

4. He is old and infirm, and quite (unable to) _____ of looking after himself.

5. Can you show me which is the most (straight and easy) _____ route to Scotland?

6. I'd like to come at 8pm tomorrow, if that's (an OK time) _____ for you, but if it's (not a good time) _____ I could come on Tuesday.

7. What is the matter with you? All those sums are (wrong) _____.

8. I think his books are quite (funny) _____ they make me laugh.

9. When we went to Mecca we stayed in a (very splendid, expensive) _____ hotel.

10. If you want that job, I can speak to my friend, he is an (person who can get people to do what he wants) _____ person on the council.

11. Please be careful with that pot, it's very (worth a lot of money) _____.

12. I couldn't manage without her, her help is (essential) _____.

13. They live in a (very dirty and poor) _____ house on the (edge) _____ of a big city.

14. That man has been (hanging around) _____ near our house for sometime. He looks (like he may be up to no good) _____.

16. You are so (un co-ordinated) _____ you are always knocking things over.

15. I (very clearly) _____ heard you say you were going to do it.

outskirts	influential	luxurious	culpable	humorous
squalid	valuable	suspicious	convenient	securely
inconvenient	polluted	invaluable	loitering	incapable
incorrect	distinctly	clumsy	direct	

Printed in Poland
by Amazon Fulfillment
Poland Sp. z o.o., Wrocław